Corporate Marriage
<u>WORKBOOK</u>
Biblical Wisdom Combined with Business Strategies
for a
Marriage That Thrives

Kyle & Tomeka Speller

KSG Enterprises, LLC

Published by KSG Enterprises, LLC
www.KSG-Enterprises.com
1st Edition

ISBN: 979-8-9944426-09 (Paperback)
ISBN: 979-8-9944426-1-6 (Workbook)
ISBN: 979-8-9944426-2-3 (eBook)
Library of Congress Control Number: 2026901222
Authors' photos © by Tyler Speller

This publication includes or is inspired by design elements and graphics created using Canva. Such elements are used in accordance with Canva's free content license or under license from Canva. © Canva. No endorsement implied.

Disclaimer
This book is intended for informational purposes only and does not guarantee specific outcomes. It is designed to support couples in pursuing healthy relationship goals, which the author and publisher make no guarantees of outcomes. It is also not a substitute for replacing any medical or psychological care, or legal advice. If you or someone you know is experiencing spousal or domestic abuse, seek immediate help from the National Domestic Violence Hotline at 1-800-799-7233. If you or your partner has been diagnosed with, or may be experiencing, a mental health condition, please seek professional assistance. The National Suicide & Crisis Lifeline is available 24/7 by dialing 988.

Printed in the United States of America.

CONTENTS

1

Begin with the End in Mind

Building a Marriage that Lasts

SECTION 1: CASTING VISION TOGETHER

"Where there is no vision, the people perish." — Proverbs 29:18

Exercise: Write the Vision – Make it Plain (Habakkuk 2:2)

Take some quiet time together and prayerfully answer the following questions:

1. **What do we want our marriage to look like in 10 years?**
   (Emotionally, spiritually, relationally)

   Write your shared vision:

   _____
   _____
   _____

2. **What kind of home environment do we want to create for ourselves and our family?**
   (Think: peace, love, discipline, joy, structure, worship)

   Write your desired home culture:

   _____
   _____
   _____

3. **What legacy do we want to leave for our children, grandchildren, or community?**
   (This could be spiritual, financial, relational, or character-based.)

   Write your legacy statement:

   _____
   _____
   _____

SECTION 2: ASSESSING YOUR BLUEPRINT THE FOUNDATION

"Therefore [whoever hears] these sayings of mine, and [does] them, I will liken him unto a wise man, which built his house upon a rock:" — Matthew 7:24

☐ Is Christ the foundation of your marriage?

☐ Do you pray together regularly?

☐ Do you make decisions together through the lens of God's Word?

Prayer Prompt:
Lord, help us to build our relationship on the solid rock of Your Word, not the sand of our emotions or the world's expectations.

THE MATERIALS

Circle the building materials you most commonly use (be honest):

Cheap Materials:
Pride – Blame – Defensiveness – Withdrawal – Scorekeeping – Silence

Quality Materials:
Love – Patience – Forgiveness – Grace – Truth – Humility – Service

Discussion Questions:

- What "cheap" materials do we tend to fall back on?
- How can we replace them with quality ones starting today?

List 3 quality materials you commit to using more intentionally:

1) _____

2) _____

3) _____

HOURS OF LABOR

Reflection:
Which of these areas are you currently neglecting or coasting in?

- ☐ Emotional Connection
- ☐ Spiritual Growth Together
- ☐ Physical Intimacy
- ☐ Quality Time
- ☐ Communication
- ☐ Fun/Play

Action Step:
Pick *one* of the above and plan a specific action to strengthen it this week.
Our action plan:

_____
_____
_____

SECTION 3: KNOWING YOUR SEASON

"To everything there is a season..." — *Ecclesiastes 3:1*

Reflection Questions:

1. What season is our marriage in right now?
(Planting, pruning, growing, resting, harvesting, rebuilding?)

2. How should we be responding in this season?
(What kind of patience, hope, or faith do we need to practice?)

Write a short prayer or declaration for your current season:

_____
_____
_____

SECTION 4: DESIGNING YOUR STRATEGY

Use the grid below to create a **Marriage Strategy Map** — small steps that support your long-term vision.

AREA	CURRENT STATE	WHAT NEEDS TO IMPROVE	FIRST STEP
Communication			
Conflict Resolution			
Intimacy (Physical/Emotional)			
Spiritual Growth			
Financial Planning			
Parenting/Legacy			

Pick one area to focus on this week and commit to ONE practical action:

_____

_____

_____

SECTION 5: SEAL IT IN PRAYER

End this session by holding hands and praying together:

Prayer Suggestion:
"Father, thank You for this vision You've given us. Help us to not just dream, but to build. Teach us to serve each other with love, build with wisdom, and trust You with the outcome. Be our Rock, our Architect, and our Foundation. In Jesus' name, Amen."

2

Corporate Governance
Leading with Love

"C*ommit [your] works unto the Lord, and [your] thoughts shall be established.."*

— Proverbs 16:3

This section walks you through **eight key areas** that every couple should address when designing a strong, faith-based Marriage Plan. Think of it as your "corporate marriage retreat"—right at your kitchen table.

---

 1. CORPORATE GOVERNANCE

Leading with Love & Mutual Respect

"The greatest among you shall be your servant." — Matthew 23:11

Reflection Questions:

- In what ways do we lead each other well?
- Are there leadership imbalances that create tension?
- How can we grow in servant leadership?

Personal Inventory (Check One Each):

Trait	Husband	Wife
Encouraging Leader	☐Yes ☐No ☐Sometimes	☐Yes ☐No ☐Sometimes
Prays Over the Family	☐Yes ☐No ☐Sometimes	☐Yes ☐No ☐Sometimes
Serves Consistently	☐Yes ☐No ☐Sometimes	☐Yes ☐No ☐Sometimes

 Together: Write 2 ways you can lead with love this week.

Example: "I will ask how I can serve you daily."

---

2. ENVIRONMENTAL ANALYSIS
Understanding the Climate of Your Marriage

Where are we right now? (Check all that apply)

☐ Newlyweds
☐ Young kids at home
☐ Financial stress
☐ Career transition
☐ Grief or healing
☐ Spiritually dry
☐ Thriving and connected
☐ Empty nest
☐ Caring for aging parents

What outside voices or influences do we need to limit?
(TV, friends, culture, social media?)

_____

What do we need more of in this season?
(Laughter, rest, intimacy, spiritual nourishment?)

_____
_____

3. HUMAN CAPITAL STRATEGY
Investing in Each Other's Growth

"Two are better than one… For if they fall, the one will lift up his fellow:…"

—*Ecclesiastes 4:9–10*

Score yourself 1–5 (1 = weak, 5 = strong):

Category	Score
We pray together	
We read or learn together	
We support each other's dreams	
We grow spiritually as a couple	

 Write 1 personal area of growth you want to pursue this season:

Ask your spouse:
"How can I support you in becoming all God has called you to be?"

---

4. MARKETING

Communicating Love Daily

" Let no corrupt communication proceed out of your mouth, but that which is good to the use of edifying, that it may minister grace unto the hearers." — Ephesians 4:29

Exercise: Love Message Inventory

Each of you answers:

The last time I felt most loved by you was:

_____

One thing I wish you said more often:

_____

One nonverbal way I feel affection is:

_____

Commit to speak your spouse's "love language" this week.

5. STATISTICS
Measuring What Matters Most

Use this check-in tool monthly or quarterly.

Checkpoint	Last Time We...	Next Goal
Prayed together		
Had a date night		
Had a meaningful conversation		
Talked about our goals		
Made love		
Resolved a conflict gracefully		

 Set 1 "Metrics That Matter" goal together for this week:

---

6. FINANCIAL ANALYSIS
Stewarding Your Money as One

"For which of you, intending to build a tower, [sits] not down first, and [counts] the cost..." — Luke 14:28

 Discussion:

What are our current financial goals? (House, savings, debt freedom, giving?)

Are we financially transparent with each other?
☐ Yes ☐ No ☐ We need to be more consistent

Action Step:

Pick one financial conversation to have this week (e.g., budget review, giving plan, savings goal).

Topic: _____

---

7. PROJECT MANAGEMENT
Working Toward Shared Dreams

"…Write the vision and make it plain…" — Habakkuk 2:2

Dream Together:

What is one God-given dream we haven't yet pursued?

What's the first small step toward building it?

Define the Roles:

Who's good at:

Planning_____

Communication_____

Budgeting?_____

Execution?_____

Use your strengths as a team—not in competition, but in complement.

---

8. OPERATIONS MANAGEMENT
Daily Habits That Sustain Love

"Let all your things be done with [love]." — 1 Corinthians 16:14

Marriage Rhythm Tracker (Weekly):

Habit	Completed This Week?
Prayed together	☐ Yes ☐ No
Laughed together	☐ Yes ☐ No
Encouraged each other	☐ Yes ☐ No
Had intentional time alone	☐ Yes ☐ No
Checked in on each other's heart	☐ Yes ☐ No

Pick 1 new habit to start this week:

_____

_____

Handling Conflict: Peace-Making Practice

When your spouse is hurting:

 I will listen before offering advice
I will say "I'm sorry" without defending
 I will ask, "What do you need from me right now?"
I will follow up after things calm down

10 Quick Words That Shift the Atmosphere

Say these daily. Especially when it's hard:

- I appreciate you
- I'm listening
- I was wrong
- I forgive you
- Thank you
- I need your help
- I missed you
- I'm proud of you
- Let's pray
- You still give me butterflies

Final Word: Let God Lead

Prayer Together:
Lord, thank You for the gift of this marriage. Help us lead with love, plan with faith, and grow with grace. Teach us to build not just a marriage, but a legacy. Let Your presence guide every strategy. In Jesus' name, Amen.

3

Environmental Analysis
Understanding the Changing Landscape of Marriage

*"S*ee *then that ye walk circumspectly, not as fools, but as wise," — Ephesians 5:15*

This workbook helps you **discern your environment**, adjust wisely, and grow stronger—together. Marriage isn't static. Seasons change. Stressors rise. Culture shifts. But when you understand your environment, you can **lead your home with spiritual clarity** and **emotional maturity.**

 ### SECTION 1: Where Are We Now?

Mark the current season(s) of your marriage (check all that apply):

- ☐ Newly married
- ☐ Raising young children
- ☐ Teen parenting
- ☐ Empty nest / retirement transition
- ☐ Career pressure / business building
- ☐ Financial strain
- ☐ Grief or healing
- ☐ High stress / low intimacy
- ☐ Growing spiritually
- ☐ Feeling stuck or distant
- ☐ Thriving in love and unity

What words describe our current marital environment?

_____
_____
_____

 ### SECTION 2: CULTURAL CHANGE — What's Influencing Us?

"She [looks] well to the ways of her household…" — Proverbs 31:27

Discussion Questions:

1.　What modern cultural shifts are subtly shaping our values, time, or intimacy?

e.g., Screen time, gender expectations, parenting trends, career hustle culture

---

2. Are we reacting to culture or intentionally shaping our home around God's truth?
   ☐ Reacting
   ☐ A bit of both
   ☐ Anchored in God's Word

3. What boundaries might we need to protect our marriage from cultural drift?

SECTION 3: ORGANIZATIONAL BEHAVIOR — How Do We Function Together?

"Can two walk together, except they be agreed?" — *Amos 3:3*

Patterns Check-In:

Pattern / Behavior	Our Reality	Needs Improvement?
We communicate daily	☐ Yes ☐ No	☐ Yes ☐ No
We serve each other well	☐ Yes ☐ No	☐ Yes ☐ No
We resolve conflict quickly	☐ Yes ☐ No	☐ Yes ☐ No
We know each other's emotional needs	☐ Yes ☐ No	☐ Yes ☐ No

Pattern / Behavior	Our Reality	Needs Improvement?
We know who handles what (roles)	☐ Yes ☐ Nc	☐ Yes ☐ No

✍️ What "unspoken rules" or habits might need to be revisited?

_____

✍️ What ONE role or pattern can we re-align this week?

_____

SECTION 4: SWOTT ANALYSIS FOR YOUR MARRIAGE
Take time as a couple to fill in each part thoughtfully.

STRENGTHS — Internal Positives
What makes us a strong team?

_____
_____
_____

WEAKNESSES — Internal Challenges
Where do we consistently struggle?

_____
_____
_____

OPPORTUNITIES — External Possibilities
What opportunities could grow us spiritually, emotionally, or relationally?

_____
_____
_____

⚠ **THREATS — External Pressures or Risks**

What is pulling us away from connection, peace, or purpose?

_____
_____
_____

↗ **TRENDS — Ongoing Shifts to Watch**

What patterns are forming (good or bad)?

e.g., More laughter, increasing resentment, declining spiritual habits

_____
_____
_____

SECTION 5: Responding to the Environment

Action Steps (Choose 2–3 Together):

☐ Have a "no phone" evening
☐ Revisit our spiritual roles at home
☐ Reassign household duties
☐ Start a joint devotional or prayer time
☐ Block out a date night
☐ Talk to a mentor couple
☐ Address an ongoing frustration with gentleness
☐ Journal gratitude daily for one another
☐ Limit media intake and increase Scripture intake

🖋 **Write a short action plan:**

"This week, we will _____

so that our marriage stays aligned and resilient."

 SECTION 6: Scripture Reflection

Choose one verse below to memorize or post in your home this week:

- *"To everything there is a season…"* — *Ecclesiastes 3:1*
- *"She [looks] well to the ways of her household…"* — *Proverbs 31:27*
- *"Behold, I will do a new thing…"* — *Isaiah 43:19*
- *"Can two walk together, except they be agreed?"* — *Amos 3:3*

 Write it here:

_____

 How does this verse apply to our current season?

Pray this together:

 *Lord, help us to understand the season we're in. Give us wisdom to notice the shifts in our culture, our family, and our hearts—and respond with grace. Teach us to function in unity, serve one another in love, and guard our home with intentionality. Let our marriage be led by You, not by trends. Make us flexible but faithful—always growing, always anchored in Christ. Amen.*

4

Human Capital
Strategy

*"**A**nd whatsoever ye do, do it heartily, as to the Lord…"* — *Colossians 3:23*

In business, people are the most valuable asset. In marriage, that person is your spouse. This workbook helps you shift your mindset
from **maintenance** to **intentional investment**—relationally, emotionally, spiritually, and practically.

SECTION 1: INTIMACY – "In-to-Me-See"
"And they were both naked, the man and his wife, and were not ashamed." — *Genesis 2:25*

Reflection Questions:

1. Do you feel emotionally safe and fully seen in your marriage?

   ☐ Always
   ☐ Often
   ☐ Sometimes
   ☐ Rarely

2. When was the last time you had an honest, undistracted conversation?

   _____

3. In what ways do you currently express non-sexual affection?

   _____

4. What helps you feel emotionally and spiritually connected to your spouse?

   _____

Connection Practices to Try This Week (Pick 2–3):

☐ "How was your heart today?" check-in
☐ A 30-second hug before bed
☐ Flirty text or playful note
☐ Pray together before sleeping
☐ Share a dream or memory
☐ Cook or walk together—no screens

☐ Answer this question at dinner: "What's one thing you appreciated about me this week?"

✐ What is one new habit we want to develop for deeper intimacy?

SECTION 2: SERVICE – Marriage as Ministry

"Let nothing be done through strife or vainglory; but in lowliness of mind let each esteem other better than themselves."— *Philippians 2:3*

Who's Your #1 Customer?
List 3 ways your spouse feels loved and served:

1. _____
2. _____
3. _____

Service Self-Check:

Statement	True	Needs Work
I listen more to understand than to reply	☐	☐
I ask how I can help, even when I'm tired	☐	☐
I don't keep score in our relationship	☐	☐
I take initiative in meeting emotional needs	☐	☐
I forgive quickly and generously	☐	☐

✐ What's one small way you could *out-serve* your spouse this week?

What's one need you have that you'd like your spouse to better understand?

SECTION 3: PERFORMANCE PILLARS OF A THRIVING MARRIAGE

We'll explore the three core areas: **Character, Contribution, Connection.** Rate and respond.

1. CHARACTER — Respect, Support, Trust

"Two are better than one… For if they fall, the one will lift up his fellow:…"
— Ecclesiastes 4:9–10

How are we doing?

Trait	Strong	Needs Growth
Mutual respect	☐	☐
Trust and follow-through	☐	☐
Celebrating each other	☐	☐
Carrying our share	☐	☐
Seeing each other as God does	☐	☐

Which trait do we most want to strengthen?

---

2. CONTRIBUTION — Focus, Dedication, Collaboration

"Can two walk together, except they be agreed?" — *Amos 3:3*

Shared Goals Check-In:

We're aligned on our goals for...

Area	Yes	Somewhat	No
Spiritual growth	☐	☐	☐
Parenting	☐	☐	☐
Finances	☐	☐	☐
Health & lifestyle	☐	☐	☐
Future vision	☐	☐	☐

Where do we need to recalibrate?

_____

What is one area where we can collaborate better starting now?

_____

_____

3. CONNECTION — Communication, Trust, Safety

"Speaking the truth in love..." — *Ephesians 4:15*
"Swift to hear, slow to speak..." — *James 1:19*

Communication Audit:

Communication Habit	Yes	Needs Work
We don't assume the worst	☐	☐
We speak directly to each other—not others	☐	☐
We resolve conflict promptly	☐	☐
We check in emotionally—not just logistically	☐	☐

What's one communication pattern we want to shift?

_____

What does "safe communication" look like for each of us?

_____

_____

SECTION 4: STRATEGIC GROWTH PLAN

Let's make a plan to steward our human capital—each other—with love and intention.

Over the next 30 days, we commit to:

One way to build intimacy:

_____

One way to out-serve each other:

_____

One way to grow in character or collaboration:

_____

One communication habit we'll practice:

_____

_____

Pray this together:

Lord, thank You for the gift of each other. Help us to see one another not through the lens of frustration or familiarity, but with the honor and reverence that love deserves. Teach us to serve joyfully, to communicate with gentleness, to connect deeply, and to walk in unity. Strengthen our character and our commitment to reflect Your heart in how we treat each other. Let our marriage be a high-performing partnership—not for applause, but for Your glory. Amen.

5

Marketing
How You Show Up in Your Marriage

*"*Let not mercy and truth forsake [you]… So [shall you] thou find favor and good understanding in the sight of God and man."* — Proverbs 3:3–4*

In business, weak branding repels people. In marriage, it slowly wears down passion. But strong marketing—showing up with consistency, thoughtfulness, and truth—builds desire, friendship, and trust. This week let's evaluate the **"brand" you're presenting at home** and make some bold upgrades.

SECTION 1: Check Your Brand Message
"You advertised 'thoughtful, fun, and present'—are you delivering on that?"

Reflection: Then vs. Now

Category	When We Were Dating	Now (Be Honest)
Affection & compliments		
Quality time		
Thoughtfulness / Surprises		
How I looked/showed up		
Emotional engagement		

What is one thing your spouse might miss about how you used to "show up"?

What's one area you want to recommit to this week?

_____

_____

SECTION 2: Reignite the Pursuit

"If you want to stay irresistible, keep investing in the pursuit."

Pick at least 3 marketing actions to do this week:

☐ Give an unprompted compliment
☐ Plan a surprise (big or small)
☐ Flirt (yes—still!)
☐ Use their love language intentionally
☐ Ask: "What would make you smile today?"
☐ Get dressed with intention, just for them
☐ Send a midday "thinking of you" message
☐ Recreate an old memory or first date moment

Bonus challenge: What's one creative thing you could do to show your spouse they're still worth pursuing?

SECTION 3: Brand Trust – Are You Delivering What You Promised?

"Let your communication be, [Yes, yes; No, no]:…" — Matthew 5:37

Statement	True	Needs Growth
I follow through on my word	☐	☐
I don't say things just to end a conversation	☐	☐
I am emotionally safe to talk to	☐	☐

Statement	True	Needs Growth
I forgive quickly and sincerely	☐	☐
I am consistent in how I show up (no hot/cold)	☐	☐

Trust Inventory:

What's one area where trust needs to be rebuilt or strengthened?

_____

What's one way your spouse has earned your trust lately?

_____
_____

SECTION 4: Communicate Like a Pro (Not a PR Crisis)

"The fruit of the Spirit is… gentleness, temperance:..." — Galatians 5:22–23

Real Talk Assessment
When conflict or stress happens, how often do you…

Habit	Often	Sometimes	Rarely
Use sarcasm or harsh tone	☐	☐	☐
Cut each other off	☐	☐	☐
Use passive-aggressive silence	☐	☐	☐
React instead of reflect	☐	☐	☐
Use timing and tone wisely	☐	☐	☐

Circle one to work on this week:

Tone | Timing | Listening | Patience | Gentleness

What will you do differently in that area?

_____

_____

SECTION 5: Non-Verbal Cues – What Is Your Body Saying?

"A merry heart [makes] a cheerful countenance:…" — _Proverbs 15:13_

Non-Verbal Self-Check:

Behavior	Consistent	Needs Work
Eye contact when listening	☐	☐
Smiling during daily moments	☐	☐
Leaning in / facing spouse fully	☐	☐
Avoiding negative gestures	☐	☐
Touch (hand on shoulder, hug, etc)	☐	☐

What does your non-verbal communication currently say about your engagement?

_____

What's one small change you can make today with your body language?

_____

SECTION 6: Show Up Plan – Building Your Irresistible Campaign

"Don't just present your best self in public—but even more so in private."

Weekly Intentions – My Marriage Marketing Plan:

Category	I Will...
Physical presence	
Emotional support	
Verbal kindness	
Trust building	
Playfulness / Joy	

Pray this together:

Lord, help us to show up for each other—not just with words, but with presence, love, and truth. Help us to communicate with kindness, to trust deeply, and to pursue each other with joy. Teach us to market who we are becoming, not just who we were. Let our marriage reflect the beauty of faithfulness and the power of love. Amen.

6

Statistics
What the Numbers are Saying

"*T*each us to number our days, that we may apply our hearts unto wisdom." – *Psalm 90:12*

In business, data tells the truth. In marriage, it's no different. Your habits are telling a story—even when you're not tracking them. This workbook will help you identify the patterns, break the cycles that don't serve you, and sow what you want to grow.

SECTION 1: Trends Don't Lie – Recognize the Patterns

"[You] shall know them by their fruits…" – Matthew 7:16

Spiritual / Emotional Metric	This Week's Score (1–10)	Notes / Reflection
Personal prayer life	_____	_____
Praying together	_____	_____
Words of affirmation given	_____	_____
Intentional quality time shared	_____	_____
Apologies made & received	_____	_____
Laughs shared	_____	_____
Acts of service (unprompted)	_____	_____

Let's track a few "marriage stats" from your recent week. Be honest.

What trend are you most encouraged by?

_____

What trend needs the most attention?

_____

_____

SECTION 2: The Seeds You're Sowing

"[Whatever] a man [sows], that shall he also reap." – Galatians 6:7

For each statement, mark how often it's true in your marriage:

IF I sow...	Often	Sometimes	Rarely
...prayer	☐	☐	☐
...patience	☐	☐	☐
...kindness in my words	☐	☐	☐
...forgiveness instead of bitterness	☐	☐	☐
...physical affection	☐	☐	☐
...focused time (no distractions)	☐	☐	☐
...respect in conflict	☐	☐	☐

If I'm honest, I've been planting more of:

[life-giving seeds]_____

[weeds] _____

What do I need to STOP planting this week?

_____

What do I want to START planting more consistently?

_____

_____

SECTION 3: Marriage Hypothesis Testing

"If I do ____, then _____ will grow in our marriage."

Craft 2–3 personal IF/THEN commitments this week based on your faith and love:

1. **If I:**_____.
   then we will _____.
2. **If I:**_____.
   then we will _____.
3. **If I:**_____.
   then we will _____.

Ask your spouse: What kind of input from me helps you feel most loved or safe?

_____

_____

SECTION 4: Spot the Outliers

"Be sober, be vigilant; because your adversary the devil, as a roaring lion, [walks] about, seeking whom he may devour." – 1 Peter 5:8

Sometimes the biggest threats don't come from bad trends—but from isolated moments we ignore. Identify any recent **outliers** (rare but meaningful moments) that need attention or repair:

⚠ Harsh words that caused hurt

⚠ Long gaps in emotional or physical connection

⚠ Growing attachment to someone outside the marriage

⚠ Moments of withdrawal or shutdown

Circle one that applies (or add your own), and write how you'll address it:

What conversation do you need to have for healing?

 SECTION 5: Marriage Metrics Dashboard
Use this weekly—or monthly—to track patterns with your spouse.

Metric	This Week	Notes / Adjustments Needed
Prayed together at least once	Y / N	_____
Shared intentional time (no phones)	Y / N	_____
Spoke each other's love language	Y / N	_____
Resolved conflict with grace	Y / N	_____
Gave an unexpected act of love	Y / N	_____
Laughed together (1–5 scale)	___ / 5	_____
Connection level (Low/Med/High)	_____	_____

Overall, are we currently trending toward:

○ More connection

○ More disconnection

○ Staying the same

What's one practical adjustment we can make this week?

Pray this together:

Lord, help us to be wise with the days You've given us. Teach us to recognize the seeds we are planting in this marriage—through our words, our actions, and our prayers. Show us where to adjust, where to repent, and where to sow with greater faith. Help us to love each other with consistency and joy. In Jesus' name, Amen.

BONUS CHALLENGE: The "7-Day Data Shift"

Pick **3 things to track daily for the next 7 days**. At the end of the week, discuss what changed.

| Metric 1: _____ |
| Metric 2: _____ |
| Metric 3: _____ |

Daily notes or checkboxes:

Day	✓ Metric 1	✓ Metric 2	✓ Metric 3	Notes
Day 1	☐	☐	☐	_____
Day 2	☐	☐	☐	_____
Day 3	☐	☐	☐	_____
Day 4	☐	☐	☐	_____
Day 5	☐	☐	☐	_____
Day 6	☐	☐	☐	_____
Day 7	☐	☐	☐	_____

7

Financial Analysis
Money, Honey & Mission

"*Two are better than one… For if they fall, the one will lift up his fellow:…*"

—*Ecclesiastes 4:9–10*

Marriage is part covenant, part calling—and your money should serve both. Let this workbook guide you through **a heart-check and a financial check**, so you can align your vision, values, and dollars.

 ### SECTION 1: Mindsets About Money

Before the math, check the mindset. Reflect on how each of you **saw money growing up** and how that might affect your current approach.

Question	Husband	Wife
Was money a source of stress or peace in your childhood?	☐ Stress ☐ Peace	☐ Stress ☐ Peace
Were your parents savers or spenders?	☐ Savers ☐ Spenders	☐ Savers ☐ Spenders
Do you feel more secure when saving or spending?	☐ Saving ☐ Spending	☐ Saving ☐ Spending
Did you talk openly about money at home?	☐ Yes ☐ No	☐ Yes ☐ No

How have these experiences shaped how you handle money in marriage?

_____

_____

_____

SECTION 2: The Marriage Money Audit

Be honest and practical. Don't just skim this—**this is your current reality.**

1. **Top 3 Financial Goals Together (Short or Long-Term)**

   1. _____
   2. _____
   3. _____

2. **Rate Your Financial Unity (1–10)**
   How well are we handling our money together?
   Score: _____ / 10

3. **Monthly Income (Net)**
   $ _____

4. **Total Monthly Expenses (Estimate)**
   $ _____

5. **Are we living:**
   - ☐ Below our means
   - ☐ At our means
   - ☐ Above our means

6. **Are we saving anything monthly?**
   ☐ Yes ☐ No — Amount: $ _____

7. **Are we tithing or giving consistently?**
   ☐ Yes ☐ No

One change we can make this month to grow in financial unity:

_____
_____

SECTION 3: Talk the Talk – Money Communication Check-In

"Can two walk together, except they be agreed?" — Amos 3:3

Discuss the following:

Topic	We're Aligned ✓	Needs Work ⚠
Spending expectations	☐	☐
Saving strategy	☐	☐
Giving priorities	☐	☐
Budgeting habits	☐	☐
Financial dreams	☐	☐
Credit card/debt use	☐	☐

What's one topic we need to revisit or clarify soon?

_____

SECTION 4: Build Your Marriage Budget Blueprint

"The thoughts of the diligent tend only to plenteousness..." — Proverbs 21:5

Let's create a starter category breakdown:

Category	Monthly Amount	Notes
Tithing / Giving	$_____	_____
Savings / Emergency Fund	$_____	_____
Debt Payments	$_____	_____

Category	Monthly Amount	Notes
Housing (Rent/Mortgage)	$_____	_____
Utilities & Bills	$_____	_____
Groceries / Food	$_____	_____
Transportation / Gas	$_____	_____
Insurance	$_____	_____
Kids / Childcare	$_____	_____
Date Nights / Fun	$_____	_____
Miscellaneous / Other	$_____	_____

Total Planned Expenses: $ _____

Is your budget balanced? ☐ Yes ☐ No ☐ Not Sure

Budgeting Note to Ourselves (about fun, margin, or discipline):

_____

_____

SECTION 5: Debt Check & Freedom Plan

"The borrower is servant to the lender." — Proverbs 22:7

What debts do we currently have?

Type of Debt	Balance	Minimum Monthly	Payoff Strategy
Credit Cards	$ _____	$ _____	_____
Student Loans	$ _____	$ _____	_____
Car Loans	$ _____	$ _____	_____

Type of Debt	Balance	Minimum Monthly	Payoff Strategy
Personal Loans	$ _____	$ _____	_____

Next Step in Our Debt Freedom Plan:

_____

Celebrate one recent WIN (no matter how small):

_____

_____

SECTION 6: Monthly Money Meeting Agenda

Use this template each month to stay in sync. Schedule 20–30 minutes.

Money Meeting Checklist:

☐ Review past month's spending
☐ Discuss upcoming bills or changes
☐ Pray over your finances
☐ Celebrate a win together
☐ Adjust any budget categories
☐ Talk about giving, saving, and fun goals
☐ Share one area you appreciate your spouse's financial effort

Notes from this month's meeting:

_____

_____

SECTION 7: Invite God Into Your Finances

"Seek ye first the kingdom of God, and His righteousness…" — *Matthew 6:33*

Pray this together:

"Lord, You are our Provider, not just our Rescuer. Help us to manage what You've given with wisdom, unity, and purpose. Teach us to give first, save diligently, and steward the rest with open hands. Remove fear, greed, or pride from our hearts, and show us how to build a financial legacy that honors You. Amen."

FINAL CHALLENGE: Build Your Kingdom Financial Culture

Check which values need more focus in your home:

Value	We're Living It ✓	Needs More Intentionality ⚠
Generosity	☐	☐
Stewardship	☐	☐
Contentment	☐	☐
Unity	☐	☐
Purpose	☐	☐

Our "Kingdom Money Motto" (create a short phrase or sentence to define how your home handles finances):

In our house, we:

8

Project Management

Building Love on Purpose

*"E*xcept the Lord build the house, they labor in vain that build it…"*
— *Psalm 127:1*

Your marriage isn't just a covenant—it's a construction site. You're building love on purpose, not luck. This workbook will help you and your spouse treat your relationship like a high-value project: planned, prayed through, executed with care, and finished in unity.

SECTION 1: Project Management in Marriage: From Vision to Victory

"Commit [your] works unto the Lord, and [your] thoughts shall be established.." — Proverbs 16:3

PART 1: Identify the Marriage Project

Every strong marriage is built intentionally. In this exercise, you will identify **one current marriage project** and manage it with clarity, wisdom, and unity.

*Name the Project

Choose **one** project you are currently facing together.

☐ Planning for a baby
☐ Paying off debt
☐ Launching a business together
☐ Resolving ongoing conflict
☐ Planning a move or major life transition
☐ Starting a joint ministry or calling
☐ Managing time and responsibilities better
☐ Rebuilding emotional and physical intimacy
☐ Other: _____

Project Name:
_____

PART 2: Clarify the Goal (Clarity Before Action)

A project without a clear goal creates frustration and confusion. Answer Together:

1. **What do we want to accomplish by working on this project?** (Be specific and shared.)

   _____

2. **How do we want our marriage to feel when this project is successful?** (Peace, closeness, trust, joy, alignment, etc.)

   _____

3. **Why does this project matter to our covenant and calling?**

   _____

PART 3: Identify the Level of Fruit for This Season

Fruit grows in stages. Wisdom is knowing **what fruit is reachable right now**.

Low-Hanging Fruit (Quick Wins)

These actions are simple, accessible, and build momentum.

Which low-hanging fruit can we harvest this week?
(Check all that apply or add your own.)

☐ Daily check-ins
☐ Prayer together (5 minutes)
☐ Holding hands / physical affection without pressure
☐ Phone-free time together
☐ Encouragement / affirmation
☐ Apology or forgiveness
☐ Other: _____

Our low-hanging fruit actions for this week:

1. _____
2. _____

Mid-Level Fruit (Intentional Effort)

These actions require planning, consistency, and teamwork.

☐ Regular date nights
☐ Honest conversations about unmet needs
☐ Creating boundaries (work, screens, schedules)
☐ Counseling, coaching, or mentorship
☐ Learning each other's love languages again
☐ Other: _____

Our mid-level fruit focus for this season:

_____

What commitment does each of us need to make?

- Spouse A commitment:

_____

- Spouse B commitment:

_____

Note:

_____

High-Level Fruit (Transformational Outcomes)

This fruit takes time, faith, and perseverance.

Which long-term fruit are we praying and working toward?
(Check any that apply.)

☐ Restored trust
☐ Emotional safety
☐ Renewed intimacy
☐ Healing from past wounds
☐ Shared spiritual vision
☐ Deep partnership and unity

What patience and faith will this require from us?

_____

PART 4: Assign Roles & Responsibilities

Projects fail when roles are unclear. Answer Together:

1. **Who is responsible for initiating next steps?**
   ☐ Spouse A ☐ Spouse B ☐ Both

2. **How will we support each other instead of blaming each other?**

   _____

3. **What boundaries or safeguards will protect unity during this process?**

   _____

PART 5: Define Progress Metrics

You can't manage what you don't measure.

How will we know we are making progress?

☐ Improved communication
☐ Reduced conflict
☐ Increased affection
☐ Greater peace at home
☐ Better teamwork
☐ Consistent follow-through

Our progress check-in schedule:
☐ Weekly ☐ Bi-weekly ☐ Monthly

PART 6: Pray and Commit the Project to God

Marriage projects are not completed by effort alone—but by grace.

Pray Together (or write your own prayer):

"Lord, we invite You into this project.
Give us wisdom, patience, humility, and unity.
Help us to start where we are, stay consistent, and trust Your
process.

We believe You are faithful to complete what You have begun in us.
In Jesus' name, Amen."

 Reflection & Commitment

- What fruit are we committing to harvest first?

- What is one action we will take within the next 24–48 hours?

- Date of next marriage project review:

Final Reminder

Marriage is not maintenance—it's management.
Strong couples don't avoid hard projects.
They manage them wisely, together, and with God at the center.

"He which hath begun a good work in you will perform it until the day of Jesus Christ:" — Philippians 1:6

SECTION 2: Walk Through the 9-Step Problem-Solving Process

Use this space to work through your chosen challenge as a couple.

Step 1: *Describe the Situation*

What's going on, honestly?

What emotions are involved?
Where might the enemy be attacking?

_____

_____

Step 2: *Frame the Right Problem*

What's the real root issue—not just the surface?

_____

_____

What happens if we don't solve it?

_____

_____

Step 3: *Describe the End-State Goals*

What does "success" look like for us?

_____

_____

How do we want to feel when this is resolved?

_____

_____

Step 4: *Identify the Alternatives*

List all possible solutions—be creative, prayerful, and honest.

    1. _____

    2. _____

    3. _____

    4. _____

Have other couples modeled healthy success in this area? (Benchmarking):

_____

_____

Step 5: *Evaluate the Alternatives*

Which of the above options helps us win *together*?

Option #	Strengths	Concerns
1		
2		
3		
4		

Values Check: Does anything violate our faith marriage values, or personal integrity?

☐ Yes ☐ No — Explain:

_____

_____

Step 6: *Identify and Assess Risks*

What could go wrong—and how can we protect our unity?

Biggest risks:

_____

What safeguards or supports can we put in place (boundaries, mentors, accountability, prayer)?

_____

_____

Step 7: *Make the Decision*

We're choosing:

✓ Option #: _____

We are in agreement: ☐ Yes ☐ Not yet
Have we prayed together about this? ☐ Yes ☐ No

Write a quick prayer of unity over the decision:
"Lord, help us stay united as we take this next step…"

_____

_____

Step 8: *Develop and Implement the Solution*
Define your project timeline and roles.
Short-term steps (Today–This Week):

_____

Mid-term steps (This Month):

_____

Who's doing what? (Split responsibilities clearly)

Task	Spouse A	Spouse B	Shared
_____	☐	☐	☐
_____	☐	☐	☐
_____	☐	☐	☐

How will we encourage each other as we go?

_____

_____

Step 9: *Evaluate the Results*
After 2–4 weeks, revisit this page.
What worked well?

_____

What would we do differently next time?

_____

How did this grow our marriage?

_____

What should we pray into next?

_____
_____

SECTION 3: Grow the Project Manager Mindset

Circle or highlight the traits each of you wants to grow in:

Trait	Want to Grow	Already Strong
Clarity	☐	☐
Communication	☐	☐
Collaboration	☐	☐
Accountability	☐	☐
Flexibility	☐	☐
Follow-through	☐	☐
Evaluation	☐	☐

One project management habit I will commit to practicing this month:

_____
_____

SECTION 4: Build with Christ as the Foreman

Jesus was the perfect planner and finisher. He counted the cost, followed the plan, finished the work.

"He which hath begun a good work in you will perform it until the day of Jesus Christ:" — *Philippians 1:6*

Write this at the top of your fridge or mirror:

"We are building our love on purpose—with God as our architect, grace as our blueprint, and unity as our daily task."

Pray together:

"Jesus, help us build this marriage with wisdom, faith, and love. Make us excellent managers of our time, energy, and purpose. Show us how to work in unity and remind us that what we're building is worth the work. Amen."

FINAL CHALLENGE: Project Review Rhythm

Create a regular rhythm for "project check-ins" as a couple:

☐ Weekly "Builder Briefings" (10–15 minutes)
☐ Monthly Marriage Planning Dates
☐ Quarterly Vision Retreats or Staycations
☐ Annual Marriage Goals Review & Prayer

9

Operations Management
Running Marriage with Purpose

"Let all things be done decently and in order."
— *1 Corinthians 14:40*

Marriage isn't just a covenant—it's a calling that requires **daily operational excellence**. This workbook helps you bring order to the areas that matter most: your habits, communication, priorities, and spiritual rhythms.

Let's build not just a strong marriage—but a *well-run* one.

 ### SECTION 1: Marriage Metrics – Measure What Matters

"You can't grow what you don't track."
Let's take inventory of your current marriage health across 8 key areas.

Rate each from 1 (low) to 5 (high), then reflect.

Metric	1–5 Rating	Notes
Prayer time together	_____	_____
Emotional/physical intimacy	_____	_____
Words of affirmation	_____	_____
Quality time	_____	_____
Conflict resolution speed	_____	_____
Forgiveness	_____	_____
Progress on shared goals	_____	_____
Laughter/fun	_____	_____

What stood out to you the most?

_____

Which 1 or 2 areas will we focus on improving this month?

_____
_____

SECTION 2: Keep an Account – Gratitude + Growth Metrics

Use this space to reflect on God's goodness and your growth as a couple.

Answered prayers we've seen:

_____

Challenges we've overcome together:

_____

Ways we've grown or matured individually and together:

_____

Moments of joy, laughter, or blessing we want to remember:

_____

Tip: Start a *Marriage Memory Bank* journal—log one entry per week!

Tip

SECTION 3: Mistake Metrics – Learn, Don't Repeat

Every misstep is a chance to realign—not a reason to shame.

Think about a recent disagreement or moment of misalignment. Answer together:

- Where did I/we go off course?

_____

- What triggered it?

_____

- What could we have done differently?

_____

- What will we try next time?

_____

Remember: Mistakes are feedback, not failure.

🏆 SECTION 4: Winning Cycle – Reinforce What's Working
Celebrate what's working—because what you *celebrate*, you *sustain*.

This past week/month…

✓ What worked well in our marriage?

✓ What did I do that made you feel seen, loved, or respected?

✓ What healthy habit or routine should we keep?

How will we celebrate progress this week? (Simple ideas: favorite dessert, prayer of thanks, date night, written love note)

👫 SECTION 5: ROI in Marriage – Invest Intentionally
Great marriages don't just happen—they're *built* through consistent investment.

Reflect and rate (1–5): Are we actively investing in these areas?

Investment Area	1–5 Rating	Small Habit to Improve
Intentional time together	___	_____
Acts of service	___	_____
Forgiveness	___	_____

Investment Area	1–5 Rating	Small Habit to Improve
Prayer together	_____	_____
Respectful communication	_____	_____
Touch and intimacy	_____	_____

One investment we commit to make this week:

_____
_____

SECTION 6: System Alignment – Syncing Strategy, People, Behavior, and Process

Answer honestly and prayerfully:

Element	Guiding Question	Our Response
Strategy	Do we have a shared spiritual vision and core values?	_____
People	Are we both showing up fully— emotionally and spiritually?	_____
Behaviors	Are our habits helping or hurting our connection?	_____
Processes	Are our routines (meals, prayer, planning, intimacy) working?	_____

What small system adjustment can we make this week to improve flow?

SECTION 7: Monthly Marriage Operations Review
Set aside 30–60 minutes monthly. Use this tool to check your marriage systems.

Review Questions:

1. What went well in our marriage this month?

   _____

2. Where did we feel tension or disconnection?

   _____

3. What habits are helping us the most?

   _____

4. What needs to change (habits, routines, communication)?

   _____

5. How did we grow spiritually together?

   _____

6. What are we proud of this month?

   _____

7. What are we looking forward to next?

   _____

Next Check-in Date: _____

_____

SECTION 8: Grace-Fueled Operations
Grace is the oil that keeps marriage systems running smoothly.

We choose to…
- ☐ Forgive quickly
- ☐ Assume the best in each other
- ☐ Speak truth in love

☐ Ask, "How can I serve you?"

☐ Trust God's timing in our growth

Prayer Together:

"Lord, help us manage our marriage with wisdom, unity, and grace. Teach us to align our actions with our purpose, and our habits with heaven. Let our home reflect Your order, joy, and peace. In Jesus' name, Amen."

10

Vision and Order in the Home

"*E*xcept the Lord build the house, they labor in vain that build it…"— *Psalm 127:1*

God isn't calling us to merely have a *house*—but to *build a home*.
A home with vision. A home with order. A home that reflects heaven.

This workbook section will help you clarify your family's purpose, confront the habits that undermine it, and cultivate a daily culture that honors God.

SECTION 1: Write the Vision — Make It Plain

"Where there is no vision, the people perish…" — *Proverbs 29:18*
"Write the vision and make it plain…" — *Habakkuk 2:2*

Reflection Prompt:
Imagine your life is complete, and your children/grandchildren are telling stories about the kind of home you built. What do you want them to say?

My Family Legacy Vision:

_____
_____
_____
_____
_____
_____

SECTION 2: Lay the Foundation — Family Vision & Values

Every strong house needs a blueprint. Use this space to craft or revise your family's vision and core values.

Our Family Vision Statement
(Who we are, what we stand for, what we're building)

_____
_____

Our Core Family Values
(Examples: Faith, Honor, Hospitality, Humility, Joy, Truth, Excellence)

1. _____
2. _____
3. _____
4. _____
5. _____

House Rules That Reflect Our Values:
(What we always do / never do, based on those values)

_____

_____

SECTION 3: Diagnose the Disorder
You can't fix what you don't name. Be honest about what's out of order.

Check any that apply:

☐ **Our schedule feels chaotic, not intentional**
☐ **We spend more time on devices than with each other**
☐ **We often react rather than lead spiritually**
☐ **We don't have consistent prayer/worship rhythms at home**
☐ **There's confusion about our priorities as a family**
☐ **We're surviving, not thriving**

What do you believe is the root cause?

_____

SECTION 4: Reclaim the Rhythm – Put Godly Order in Place
"Let all things be done decently and in order." — 1 Corinthians 14:40

Use this section to design simple systems of order that reflect Kingdom priorities.

Spiritual Rhythms
When and how do we pray/worship as a family?

_____

Relational Rhythms
How do we connect regularly as a couple?

_____

Practical Systems
Budgeting / Financial Stewardship Plan:

_____

How do we create joyful time with our children?

_____

Chores / Household Responsibilities:

_____

Weekly Planning Routine (calendar check-in, rest day, meals, etc.):

_____

_____

SECTION 5: Priorities Audit – Is Our Order God's Order?

God's design is simple:
1. **God first**
2. **Spouse second**
3. **Children third**
4. **Everything else afterward**

Evaluate honestly:

Area	In Right Order? (✓ / X)	Needs Attention
My walk with God	____	_____
My marriage	____	_____
My parenting	____	_____
My work	____	_____
My hobbies/social life	____	_____
Ministry/church service	____	_____

What needs to change for your home to reflect God's order?

_____

SECTION 6: Vision Communication Plan

A vision only works if it's shared.

✓ Have we talked about our family vision together?
✓ Do our kids know what our family is about?
✓ Do we live out our values in visible, daily ways?

Ways we will begin to communicate and reinforce our vision:

- _____ Family mission/vision written and displayed in home
- _____ Weekly family devotion or prayer night
- _____ Regular "family table" conversations about values
- _____ Stories, photos, or traditions that reinforce our identity

Notes:

_____

SECTION 7: Reverse Engineer Your Legacy

"Vision without habits is a fantasy. Vision with habits is transformation."

If your end goal is:

- A peaceful, faith-filled home
- A Christ-centered marriage
- Kids who walk with God

Then what habits must you build today?

Legacy Goal	Daily/Weekly Habit
_____	_____
_____	_____
_____	_____

SECTION 8: Final Reflection + Prayer
Vision Check-In Questions:

- What does "home" feel like to the people who live in it?

_____

- What spiritual legacy are we building?

_____

- What area of our home is most out of order right now?

_____

- What's one thing I can do this week to bring more God-honoring order to our home?

Prayer Together:

Lord, help me not to win everywhere else and lose at home.
Help me to see You in my marriage, in my parenting, and in my house.
Help me to manage my home like a kingdom assignment—not a side project.
Give me a vision that outlives me and a love that never runs dry.
In Jesus' name, Amen.

11

"I Love You"
(Four Ways)

*"W*e love Him, because He first loved us." *— 1 John 4:19*

Saying "I love you" is easy.
Living "I love you" is holy.

This section will help you identify where you are in your love journey, invite God into your relationship in a deeper way, and build a plan for lasting love rooted in truth—not just feelings.

SECTION 1: What Stage of Love Are We In?

"To everything there is a season…" — Ecclesiastes 3:1

Read each description below. Then, honestly assess where your marriage is right now.

Stage 1: Infatuation – "I Love You" (The Honeymoon Phase)
✓ Easy attraction, excitement, and enjoyment
✗ No real sacrifice yet

Stage 2: Question – "I *Think* I Love You?"
✓ Growing awareness of differences
✗ Doubts, confusion, maybe even disillusionment

Stage 3: Conflict – "I Love You, But I'm Mad!"
✓ Tension, disagreements, testing boundaries
✗ Opportunity for growth—*if* handled well

Stage 4: Agape – "I Love You – Still, Always, Anyway"
✓ Commitment over convenience
✗ Choosing love through faith, maturity, and service

Which stage best describes where we are today?

Why do you think we're in that stage? What has helped or hindered our growth?

 **SECTION 2: Deepen the Meaning of "I Love You"**

Love matures when it's expressed *on purpose*.

For each stage, write down how you currently express love—and how you *could* grow in it.

Stage	Current "I Love You" Examples	How I Can Grow in Love
Infatuation	_____	_____
Questioning	_____	_____
Conflict	_____	_____
Agape	_____	_____

SECTION 3: Build a Marriage Plan (Yes, Really)

"Through wisdom is an house [built]; and by understanding it is established." — Proverbs 24:3

Great marriages don't happen by accident. Let's get intentional.

Marriage Vision Statement
(What do we want our marriage to stand for?)

_____

_____

Marriage Core Values
(Examples: Faithfulness, Unity, Forgiveness, Joy, Service, Intimacy)

1. _____
2. _____
3. _____

Weekly Check-In Rhythm
(When will we stop and ask: *How are we doing?*)

_____

Conflict Recovery Plan
(What should we each do when things go wrong?)

_____

_____

Spiritual Habits Together
(Prayer, worship, study, devotionals, church attendance)

_____

_____

SECTION 4: Express Love in Action

Agape love is lived more than spoken. Choose **3 ways** to intentionally show love this week:

☐ Write a handwritten letter or affirmation note
☐ Plan a surprise date or shared moment
☐ Pray over your spouse out loud
☐ Do one unexpected act of service
☐ Apologize first in a lingering conflict
☐ Speak your spouse's love language
☐ Create space for open, judgment-free conversation
☐ Other: _____

Which ones will I commit to this week?

_____

_____

 **SECTION 5: Reflection Questions**

What does "I love you" mean to me *now* vs. when we got married?

_____

When do I feel the most loved by my spouse?

_____

How can we better reflect God's love to each other daily?

_____

What part of our love needs healing, growth, or fresh perspective?

_____
_____

SECTION 6: The Covenant Reminder

Re-read your wedding vows or write a fresh one below to recommit your heart:

My Covenant Commitment to You (Fresh Vow):

I choose you today—still, always, and anyway.
Through joy and pain, wins and losses, I will honor our promise.
I will love, forgive, serve, and grow with you.
I'm not here just for the easy days—I'm here for *every* day.
And with God's help, I will love you like Christ loves His Church.
Amen.

(*Add your own personal line if you'd like):

_____
_____

Prayer Together

Father, thank You for the gift of love and the covenant of marriage. Give us the courage to love in every season: through excitement, through questions, through conflict, and into agape. Teach us to live "I love you" in how we speak, serve, forgive, and grow. Let our marriage reflect Your heart—steadfast, sacrificial, and full of grace. In Jesus' name, Amen.

12

Trinergy

The Power of a Threefold Partnership

"T hough one may be overpowered, two can defend themselves. A cord of three strands is not quickly broken." — Ecclesiastes 4:12

This workbook section is designed to help you move **Trinergy** from concept to practice. You will reflect, discuss, assess your current dynamics, and intentionally invite God into the center of your marriage systems.

PART 1: PERSONAL REFLECTION

Individual Exercise (Answer Separately)

Take a few moments to answer honestly. Do not compare answers yet.

1. When I think about my marriage right now, I would describe our current strength as:
☐ Fragile ☐ Stable ☐ Growing ☐ Strong ☐ Thriving

2. I feel closest to my spouse when:

---

3. I feel closest to God when:

---

4. One area where I tend to rely on myself instead of God in our marriage is:

---

5. One strength I believe God has given me that benefits our marriage is:

PART 2: UNDERSTANDING THE TRIANGLE (TRINERGY MODEL)

The Three Roles

- **God (The Apex):** Vision, truth, stability, grace, direction
- **Husband:** Leadership, covering, responsibility, sacrifice
- **Wife:** Wisdom, partnership, nurturing, strength

Trinergy is not hierarchy—it is alignment.

Discussion Questions

Answer together:

1. Where do we currently place God in our decision-making (top, consulted, or optional)?
2. In what areas do we function as two strands instead of three?
3. How does drawing closer to God practically bring us closer together?

Write your shared insights below:

_____
_____
_____

PART 3: SYNERGY vs. TRINERGY CHECK

Circle the statement that best reflects your marriage today:

- We work well together, but often without prayer.
- We include God during crisis, but not consistency.
- God is actively involved in our daily decisions.

Reflection

What would need to change for God to move from *invited guest* to *central architect* in your marriage?

_____
_____

PART 4: MARRIAGE DYNAMICS ASSESSMENT

Identify Your Current Dynamic

(Check all that apply)

☐ Pursue / Withdraw
☐ Lead / Resist
☐ Protect / Avoid
☐ Collaborate / Support
☐ Pray / Plan Together

Reflection

Which dynamic strengthens your marriage? Which weakens it?

_____

_____

PART 5: FROM DYNAMICS TO TRINAMICS

Marriage Trinamics occur when God actively governs:

- Communication
- Conflict resolution
- Roles and responsibilities
- Vision and future planning

Exercise: Reframe One Dynamic

Choose one recurring issue (finances, intimacy, time, parenting, conflict).

Current Dynamic:

_____

What We Usually Do:

_____

How God's Presence Changes This:

_____

_____

PART 6: ALIGNMENT ACTION PLAN

This Week's Trinergy Commitments

We commit to pray together:

☐ Daily ☐ 3x this week ☐ Once intentionally

One decision we will bring before God together this week:

_____

One habit we will adjust to better reflect God-centered unity:

_____

_____

PART 7: THREEFOLD CORD DECLARATION

(Read aloud together)

We declare that our marriage is not built on effort alone, but on God's presence.
As we draw near to Him, He draws us closer to one another.
Our marriage is strengthened, aligned, and sustained by Trinergy.

_____

CLOSING PRAYER

Lord, today we invite You fully into the center of our marriage. Align our hearts, order our steps, and strengthen our bond. Teach us to function not merely in synergy, but in Trinergy—where You are our source, our guide, and our strength. Bind us together with a threefold cord that cannot be broken. Amen.

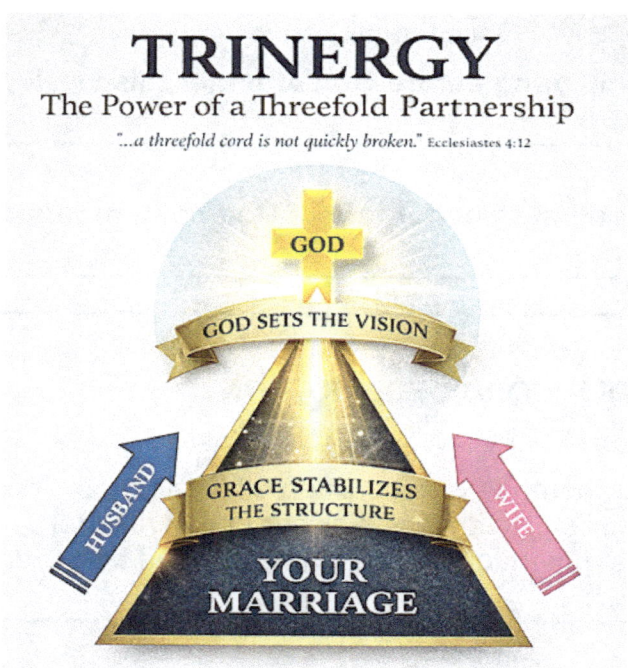

"For other foundation can no man lay than that is laid, which is Jesus Christ."
~1 Corinthians 3:11

Certificate of Achievement

This certificate recognizes the dedication and hard work necessary to complete this important journey:

Mr. _____

&

Mrs./Miss _____

Together, they attained a

Marriage Business Administration (MBA)

Certificate

This couple has diligently completed the activities outlined in the *Corporate Marriage Workbook* and are better equipped for the mission and responsibilities of marriage.

(Ephesians 5:21-33)

Earned on: _____
date

REFERENCES & ACKNOWLEDGEMENTS

Unless otherwise indicated, *Scripture quotations from The Authorized (King James) Version. Rights in the Authorized Version in the United Kingdom are vested in the Crown. Reproduced by permission of the Crown's patentee, Cambridge University Press.*

Chapman, Gary. *The 5 Love Languages: The Secrets to Love that Lasts.* Chicago: Northfield Publishing, 1992

About the Authors

Photo by © Tyler Speller

Kyle obtained two Master's Degrees – Business Administration and Strategic Human Resources with Learning and Development Concentration. He is a man deeply devoted to his family, his faith, and his craft. His love for voice work began in college as a campus disk jockey. Over the years, he developed his talent and now works as a professional Public Address Announcer for a pro sports team, with his voice also featured in national commercials and events. Spiritually rooted, Kyle has served as a Youth Pastor, Urban Director, Associate Pastor, and Team Chaplain. His heart for service extends into community outreach and volunteer efforts across Denver. Kyle's greatest joy is spending quality time with his wife and their three children and granddaughter.

Tomeka holds a Bachelor's in Human Services & Management and a Master's in Marriage and Family Therapy. Also rooted in her Faith, she has worked with individuals and families affected by trauma, domestic violence, and systemic challenges. Tomeka has designed and led support groups & workshops, and her passion for guiding people through life transitions, brings both professional expertise and personal insight to her work.